START-UP INSPIRATIONS
FROM DREAMS TO REALITY

RAHAYU TASNIM
MAIZAITULAIDAWATI MD HUSIN
OBED RASHDI SYED
ZARINA ABDUL SALAM

INDIA · SINGAPORE · MALAYSIA

Notion Press

Old No. 38, New No. 6
McNichols Road, Chetpet
Chennai - 600 031

First Published by Notion Press 2018
Copyright © Rahayu Tasnim, Maizaitulaidawati Md Husin, Obed
Rashdi Syed, Zarina Abdul Salam 2018
All Rights Reserved.

ISBN 978-1-64429-707-0

This book has been published with all efforts taken to make the material error-free after the consent of the author. However, the author and the publisher do not assume and hereby disclaim any liability to any party for any loss, damage, or disruption caused by errors or omissions, whether such errors or omissions result from negligence, accident, or any other cause.

No part of this book may be used, reproduced in any manner whatsoever without written permission from the author, except in the case of brief quotations embodied in critical articles and reviews.

Contents

Preface — v
About the Editors — vii
List of Writers — ix
Acknowledgement — xi

1. **BIOGAS AND SOLAR SERVICE PROVIDER** — 1
   Obed Rashdi Syed

2. **SPEAK EAZY: PUBLIC SPEAKING PROGRAMME FOR UNDERPRIVILEGED KIDS** — 17
   Maizaitulaidawati Md Husin & Nazimah Hussin

3. **TOO FAST AND FURIOUS? A MALAYSIAN MAVERICK'S BLOCKCHAIN SAGA** — 27
   Rahayu Tasnim

4. **IMAGINARY PAY** — 45
   Zarina Abdul Salam

5. **MALAYSIA RARE DISORDERS SOCIETY (MRDS): A GOLDEN CITIZEN'S STRUGGLE** — 55
   Muhammad Nizam Zainuddin & Obed Rashdi Syed

Preface

Venturing into an innovative start up demand not only unique strategies, efficient resources, and more importantly, a burning will power to survive the first few years in business. Suitable for a light reading while over a cup of hotly brewed tea, the start-up cases narrated in this book will empower and drive you into understanding the behaviors and special characteristics of nascent entrepreneurs, i.e. why do they do things that seemed illogical an surreal? Why do they act sui generis? What drives them to do so? And what do they think of when faced with failures? These five mini cases portrays real life stories of five start up entrepreneurs who dream to make it big one day, in their own unique ways. At this point, all five start-ups are running their businesses in Kuala Lumpur, two of which are already global market players.

About the Editors

Rahayu Tasnim

A PhD holder in Entrepreneurial Psychology, dynamic researcher and charismatic business consultant, as well as a corporate trainer in self-development and entrepreneurship related modules, Rahayu is with 19-solid years of both academic and industry experiences, having first attached to the Port of Tanjung Pelepas and Takaful Nasional, handling Corporate Communications and Marketing, prior to holding academic positions in four renowned private universities in Malaysia, of which her last post, as the Vice President Academic and Provost. Rahayu is at present holding a Senior Lectureship position in the Azman Hashim International Business School of Universiti Teknologi Malaysia, a renowned Research-University in the region, and am tasked to bridge the academia-industry gap with impactful networking and industrial relations, benefiting the university, industry and community as a whole. In 2017, Rahayu championed the Swiss Innovation Challenge Asia Project, a 9 month mentoring program mentoring innovative start-ups, 5 of which detailed here in this book.

Maizaitulaidawati Md Husin

Currently a senior lecturer at Azman Hashim International Business School of Universiti Teknologi Malaysia, Maizaitul had a successful career in banking before fulfilling her dream of becoming a lecturer. Now with more than 8 years of experience in teaching, research and supervision, she has authored and co-authored various book chapters, articles and research papers in journals and conference proceedings. She is also actively writing business case studies. Her current research interest includes Islamic banking and finance, takaful, Islamic economics, Islamic marketing, behavioural finance, and consumer behaviour. Visit her profile at https://www.maizaitulaidawati.com/

Obed Rashdi Syed

Obed Rashdi Syed is a senior lecturer at Azman Hashim International Business School of Universiti Teknologi Malaysia (UTM-AHIBS).. He earned his PhD from UTM-AHIBS in 2017. His research area is human resource development. He has published research on business education and academic-industry collaboration.

Zarina Abdul Salam

Zarina started her career as a senior executive in Bank Negara Malaysia. She performed audit supervision of all financial institutions in Malaysia to ensure that they complied with the Banking Acts and regulations. She currently registered as chartered accountants with Malaysian Institute of Accountant. She pursued MBA and PhD and started her career as a senior lecturer in Universiti Teknologi Malaysia. She supervised research apart from teaching MBA and PhD program. She is the author and the co-author of several books and book chapters, articles, journals, conference proceedings and case studies. Her research interests cover several aspects which are financial reporting quality, corporate governance, corporate disclosure, audit, corporate issues and corporate performance.

List of Writers

Maizaitulaidawati Md Husin

Muhammad Nizam Zainuddin

Nazimah Hussin

Obed Rashdi Syed

Rahayu Tasnim

Zarina Abdul Salam

Acknowledgement

First and foremost, all praises be to Allah, the Almighty, the most merciful the most benevolent for His guidance and blessings for giving us the inspiration and opportunity to embark on this project and to make this dream a reality.

Many people have contributed to the creation and completion of this book. We would like to express our gratitude to all authors who made this book a success. We also express our humble gratitude to the business owners who have provided their invaluable information to write about their company background and issues. We are indebted to those who provided us their support and feedback to improve the quality of this book. The special appreciation goes to our family members for their unconditional love and support to allow us to devote ourselves to the completion of this book. Finally, we thank the Swiss Innovation Challenge Asia 2017 (Malaysia) Team for the exciting opportunity in this inaugural publication.

Rahayu Tasnim
Maizaitulaidawati Md Husin
Obed Rashdi Syed
Zarina Abdul Salam

Biogas and Solar Service Provider

Founder	:	Yusniman Bin Lotfi
Nationality	:	Malaysian
Age of the founder at start-up	:	47
Education	:	BSc Electronics
Professional background	:	Technical Manager
Family background	:	Teaching
Business type	:	Renewable Energy
Business partners	:	Adam Rizal Azwar and Samsuddin Bin Zainal
Country of operation	:	Malaysia
Year of start-up	:	2017

Written by:
Obed Rashdi Syed

INSPIRATION TOWARDS THE BUSINESS STARTUP

With interest, education and experience in electronic engineering, Yusniman and his friend Adam Rizal founded a company called *Techbrain PLT*. They patented the *Grid View* technology, a non-intrusive image-capturing with image recognition technology, and presented their prototype at an international competition held in Malaysia in 2017. The team did not manage to get an award in the competition, but this experience provoked Yusniman to start a new business in the renewable industry.

"Looking at the fact that about 10 thousand tonnes of food are wasted every day... The landfill in Malaysia is increasing."

Yusniman started looking into the aftermath effects of food wastage and air pollution that are caused by the late-night vegetable markets and food streets in many cities in Malaysia. Many food and vegetable stalls in the late-night markets mainly rely on portable gasoline electricity generators which are *"noisy and populous"* to the nearby residents or shops in the market area. These markets also produce a huge amount of waste which damages public streets, produces unpleasant smell, and increases the garbage collectors' workload, whilst increasing landfills which have harmful effects on our environment.

"When you throw [wet waste] at the landfill it will create an odour, bad odour, create ... methane gas. That methane gas contributes to the greenhouse effect."

There are many companies that recycle solid waste like plastic, metal, paper, glass, etc. But the remaining waste like leftover food, vegetables and fruits are contributing in increasing the greenhouse effects and fetid landfills. According to Yusniman, solid waste counts for around 60% of the total waste; the remaining 40% of the waste is "*wet waste*". That waste is problematic as there are not many companies recycling it. Therefore, he and his friend Samsuddinfounded another company named *Persada Efektif Sdn. Bhd.* to sell two products that could reduce air pollution and recycle that remaining 40% of the waste.

THE BUSINESS PRODUCTS

The first product that he imported from China is the battery powered electricity Genset. This Genset is rechargeable using electric supply or solar energy panels. He also imports a portable solar lightening system which includes a set of LED bulbs, a small lithium battery and connecting wires to light up a room or a small house. Both these electric products are meant not only for the late-night markets in the metropolitan cities but also for the populace of remote areas where electricity supply is not available. For instance, they collaborated with a few NGOs that were aiding refugees in Bangladesh by providing them portable tents and other basic resources. Yusniman offered those NGOs the solar lightening system to facilitate the refugees. For the electric Genset, the target customers are also travellers who explore rural areas and need a portable electricity supply system.

"So this is my first activity on renewable solar energy which is operating but not in a big scale."

Solar Lightning System

The second product that Yusniman and his partner imported from China is the anaerobic digester. Samsuddin was initially involved in the business of crunching the wet waste to produce fertiliser for farming. However, Yusniman and Samsuddin explored the other uses of wet waste through the internet and found that there are actually three different outputs that they could possibly produce from the wet waste, namely fertiliser, methane gas, and electricity. All they needed was a proper system to process these outputs, and the anaerobic digester is a major equipment of this system.

"The output of this equipment, anaerobic digester. ...One is the fertiliser, number two is a
gas, number three the gas can be fitted into a gas generator and produces in electricity."

Yusniman in front of an Unassembled Anaerobic Digester Unit

BRINGING BUSINESS IDEAS INTO PRACTICE

The business of importing the Genset and solar power system is not very complex; Yusniman just orders these products from China and sells it to local individual customers and companies. However, in the business of converting waste into biogas, fertiliser and electricity, there are several issues that need to be tackled. For instance, getting the required wet waste from different sources, installing the anaerobic digester at the right place, and finding customers for these products. In addition, at the organisational level, there is a need for a partner; a companion who is reliable and equally passionate about the business.

"There is always a partner, a guy, a friend that has an idea and is looking for somebody to share it with. So in my case, I have a friend, Mr. Samsuddin."

After exploring business ideas and discussing with Samsuddin, Yusniman reached the national authority for renewable energy in Malaysia named 'SEDA' for their advice. SEDA appreciated his ideas and informed him about funds for renewable energy projects, and the way to get feed-in tariff from Tenaga Nasional (TN – national electricity supplier); if TN is properly convinced to buy the electricity he produces through biogas. SEDA also suggested him to test his ideas in a remote area before implementing them in the cities. SEDA particularly suggested running a trial project in Langkawi – a tourist destination that has issues of limited landfills and an increasing need of electricity.

"SEDA authority advised us to set this up in one area, which is the Langkawi Island. Because in an island you need to manage the waste."

Following SEDA's advice, Yusniman went to discuss this business idea with the waste management authority called E-edaman in Langkawi, and they agreed to give him the wet waste collected from a particular area.

"There is one company, E-edaman. ... They collect the waste. ... So I tell them that I don't want to touch on the solid waste; you do your own job, you collect your bottles, plastic, everything, but for the wet waste, organic waste, I want that waste."

To enhance the input of ideas and feasibility of bringing those ideas into practice, he came into contact with the renewable energy centres of two public universities for resource support. He contacted a few local NGOs, such as MAMPAN, to install anaerobic digesters in different areas in Malaysia.

FUNDING THE BUSINESS

Yusniman's main interest is to produce methane gas and electricity using wet waste, whereas his partner Samsuddin is interested in fertilisers produced from wet waste. Their first trial project in Langkawi is primarily funded through personal savings. The project startup at this stage costed them about RM10,000 (Malaysian ringgit). However, for a bigger scale project like this in bigger cities, it could cost them up to RM200,000.

"We only invested RM10,000 to prepare the platform, and also for the operational costs to go to Langkawi, because we have a few meetings ... meet the authorities for the approval."

SEDA informed Yusniman that the energy providers in Malaysia reserve trust funds in SEDA's account and they use that money to fund small-scale, green projects like this. But they need to prove that the project works in practice. With that in mind, Yusniman and his partner are planning to extent their project in other areas of Langkawi with funding support from SEDA after successfully running the trial project and producing electricity and fertilisers.

"I am going to prepare this in Langkawi still ... in multiple places with the fund by SEDA."

Yusniman was also in touch with the Selangor state government's renewable energy centre to get funds for this project. The state government provides RM10,000 for renewable energy projects. So, he presented his ideas and showed the results of their on-going successful trails in Langkawi, and he succeeded in acquiring the grant. In a similar way, he was also trying to reach different NGOs working within and outside Malaysia to share his ideas and get financial support to extend his business scope.

COMPETITORS IN THE RENEWABLE INDUSTRY

The renewable industry is still at its infancy stage in Malaysia and there are not many companies working on green energy projects. However, Yusniman believes that there are at least two *"players"* in Malaysia who are working in this business and he would rather learn from them. One of the regulatory bodies called the *Standard and Industrial Research Institute of Malaysia* (SIRIM) has already installed anaerobic digesters at two different places near Kuala Lumpur, and they have plans to extend their project to other parts of the city.

"Instead of competing, since they are a government body, we learn from them."

SIRIM and other similar bodies are already producing biogas, fertilisers and electricity using the anaerobic digester system. However, the market is still open for new players as more than 75% of the market remains *"untapped"*, according to Yusniman. There are several other areas in Malaysia where there is a need to recycle the wet waste into something useful. Rather than considering these companies as competitors, Yusniman believes that he would reach them, offer them a partnership, and expand their share of the pie.

MARKETING STRATEGIES

The marketing strategy at the startup stage for Yusniman is *"good networking"*. Since the business is small and with limited resources, they have to develop good relationships with all those who are already established and working at a bigger scale.

"Being small, we need to create repo and link with all the big guys, at the same time we protect our interests."

With this objective at the frontline, Yusniman started making connections with SEDA, E-edaman, and Majlis Perbandaran Langkawi (the town municipal of Langkawi). The networking strategy enabled Yusniman to develop an understanding with all the concerned authorities and get initial support and resources to fuel his business.

Yusniman believes that this business of converting wet waste into biogas and electricity through the anaerobic digester system requires different parties to collaborate. It is a supply-chain process whereby involvement of companies like Alam-Flora (a waste collector company in Selangor) and E-edaman is needed to separate the solid and the wet wastes, and SEDA and Indah Water (water supply management) are required to help develop the quality of slurry needed to power the anaerobic digester to perform at its best capacity.

"When they don't talk to each other, they will be in silo, and then the whole process doesn't work."

When these big firms are synergised, they will be able to manage the wet waste and constantly supply the slurry made up of the wet waste. That slurry will provide the input for renewable energy organisations to effectively produce fertilisers, methane gas and electricity.

STRENGTHS OF THE COMPANY

Yusniman believes that the smallness and entrepreneurial outlook stand as strengths of the company. Certainly, at this stage there are inadequate resources and the startup is encountering several challenges to grow. However, the advantage of having less management issues and no bureaucratic procedures enabled Yusniman and his partner to make quick decisions and changes in the product presentation to fit a potential customer's requirements.

"Being small means being dynamic... we can change the presentation overnight, very fast. We don't need to refer to a lot of management; there is less bureaucracy, I just discuss with my colleague. ... We can quickly make decisions because there are only the two of us."

Yusniman's partner Samsuddin has been in the business of renewable energy since 2015. He was mainly interested in converting the wet waste into organic fertilisers, and he used to work on a waste-cruncher machine with a few other partners in Penang, Malaysia. In addition, he used to import chemical microbes from Thailand and sold in Malaysia. Yusnimanrealised that much of the preliminary network is already established by Samsuddin. When both partnered, they explored business ideas through the internet and contacted the concerned authorities for support. Therefore, Yusniman believes that a reliable partner is also the greatest strength.

"Before the business really sells and succeeds, you need to do a lot of groundwork, have a sold background, build relationship ... know your suppliers, so luckily he already did that."

Yusniman (R) and Samsuddin at a recycle centre in Penang

CHALLENGES ENCOUNTERED

For the startup, the first and utmost issue was acquiring adequate financial resources. Yusniman was very much concerned about the fund to cover the expenses of developing the prototype, documentation and travelling. He has invested his personal savings in the startup. The gradual increase of the need of funds caused him to hunt for alternative activities that produced capital. So, he started finding consultation opportunities on electronic designs at different organisations. At the same time, he kept on meeting and making new contacts with the relevant authorities to explore funding opportunities; for instance, SEDA.

"One is the financial challenge, which we manage overcome by taking from various sources."

The second challenge for Yusniman was to convince his family to compromise on his busy schedule and limited financial support until his business grows up to the profitable stage. Constant monthly income is very much expected by every family, and the pressure was felt by Yusniman too. He said that financial challenges continued up to six months.

"You work to have income for your family, but unfortunately the process required some time."

Yusniman also experienced the issue of trust when dealing with suppliers. There were a few suppliers whom he knew personally; some were known through friends and others were new in his contact list. Those who were known were trusted him and they considerably understood that his business is a startup he is looking for a compromising deal on prices and credit terms. New contacts were reluctant to offer him payment in installments and negotiated on prices. For these suppliers, he had to arrange the required cash to avoid unforeseen problems.

"An entrepreneurial startup doesn't work from 8 to 5. Especially the founder who needs to be creative and explore the challenges and think about the project sometimes at night."

Time management is always a concern for the entrepreneurial startup. There is no fixed time like 8 to 5 work hours every day. Yusniman had to reschedule meetings and commitments with family when called by potential customers. There were times whereby he had to work continuously up to 15 hours in a day, and the presentation could not convince the customers and offers were rejected. He had to digest bitter responses and took them as an experience.

ADVICE TO NOVICE ENTREPRENEURS

The first advice for startup entrepreneurs is to carefully understand their business eco-system. Eco-system is the interconnected network system of the business, including the entire demand-supply relationship chain. The startup business would run successfully when the eco-system is comprehensively known to the entrepreneur. In addition, those players who are linked to this eco-system should also know and understand the importance of their role in the network system.

"Understanding your ecosystem will give you the understanding of where is the opportunity."

In his case, the eco-system is proper waste management that includes waste collection and separation of wet and solid waste, and conversion of the wet waste into fertilisers, biogas and electricity. Sometimes, the absence of one player in the eco-system impedes the network to complete its chain process. The renewable energy projects are already working at their edge; on the other hand, the electricity suppliers are also working, and so do the biogas and fertiliser companies. Adding one player in between connects these different players to produce cost-effective and environment-friendly outcomes.

"I don't want to make enemies, I want to empower them."

The second advice he gave to new entrants is to identify and befriend those who are indignant at your startup business. Usually, business people annoy those who are a potential threat to their businesses; assuming that the new entrant will take a piece of their share of the pie. When Yusniman started his business, he found that the waste collectors may not appreciate his business idea of reducing the weightage of the waste, which will eventually reduce their pie share. Therefore, he went with a proposal to the waste collectors and offered them more income if they properly separate the waste and sell the wet waste to him. In this way, he managed to change his competitor's perception and obtained the input needed to power up the anaerobic digester.

Speak Eazy: Public Speaking Programme for Underprivileged Kids

Founder	:	Major Dr. Prebagaran Jayaraman
Nationality	:	Malaysian
Age of the founder at start-up	:	51
Education	:	PhD in Engineering Business Management
Professional background	:	Former Education Officer of Malaysian Armed Forces Corp; Head of Marine Technology Academy, Boustead Naval Shipyard in Lumut, Perak; Co- founder and CEO of SMC Trainers Malaysia.
Business type	:	Learning and Development
Country of operation	:	Malaysia
Year of start-up	:	2016
Website	:	https://prebagaran.com/

Written by:
Maizaitulaidawati Md Husin & Nazimah Hussin

ABOUT THE FOUNDER

A person cannot be said to be fully contented when he/she only focuses on his/her own self-interest. Dr. Praba is not only soft-hearted, but also full with feelings of giving and empowering others. He is also very passionate about teaching and learning. The way he was brought up has made him determined to reach out to underprivileged kids. Thus, the CEO of Samudera Management Consultants Sdn. Bhd. has created a programme called Speak Eazy as a CSR initiative by his own firm with the noble thought of providing a voice and platform for underprivileged kids. Dr. Praba was born in a rubber estate in Padang Rengas, Perak, and was raised in a loving environment by parents who were dedicated to provide the best education despite their financial difficulty. Although coming from a less fortunate background, Dr. Praba had managed to become a teacher in 1989. During his teaching years, he met many underprivileged kids that he wanted to help out; however, his efforts were limited by the resources available. Later in 1993, he joined the Malaysian Armed Forces as an Education Officer.

Major Dr. PrebagaranJayaraman, the founder of SpeakEazy

For the last 28 years, his core business has been helping individuals and organisations to optimise their potential.

With the experiences he has, he believes that it is time for him to contribute to the society. As he believes that individuals should make continuous contributions to the society, he has chosen under privileged kids as his main focus in giving back to the society. Dr. Praba has developed a team which consists of Uma Shangery Aruldass, Pavithra Maniam, Tarcayani Prebagaran and Priyaa Tharisiny Aruldass, core members and fellow humans who have the similar passion with him to establish Speak Eazy.

STARTING OUT

Having the same aspirations, Dr. Praba and his team had discussed the various approaches that could be adopted to bridge the gap in teaching. They took an initiative by conducting several meetings with a few teachers who teach English as a core subject. They came to a conclusion that there are lots of potential to sharpen students' public speaking skills. However, the teachers interviewed had stated some challenges they face in further sharpening students' skills, such as being burdened with the syllabus and other curricular and administrative activities.

The team then took an initiative by conducting a discussion with a group of experts in public speaking from the Samudera Toastmasters Club of Lumut, Perak. Toastmasters is known as a non-profit educational organisation that is dedicated to enhance people's public speaking and leadership skills globally since 1924. The discussion had introduced the team to the Gavel Club, a club dedicated to develop the public speaking skills of children below 18 years old.

SPEAKEAZY

Initially started up as corporate social responsibility under Samudera Management Consultant (SMC), Speak Eazy has set an objective of reaching underprivileged kids who are neglected by their parents. Underprivileged children were chosen as the target market due to the fact that these kids experience difficulties in attending such public speaking programmes due to financial constraints, despite the abundancy of such programmes available.

The pilot project for Speak Eazy was conducted at a home for underprivileged children in Sitiawan, Perak from September to December 2016. The participants consisted of 20 kids ranging from 5 to 16 years old. The result of this pilot project reinforced the core members' initial assumption that these children need the basic skills of public speaking.

The second batch of the Speak Eazy programme involved 120 teenagers ranging from 13 to 16 years old who live at the Educational, Welfare and Research Foundation Malaysia (EWRF) centre in Kajang. The programme was conducted for 6 months starting from October 2017. Several activities were conducted, including boot camp. Facilitated by 12 volunteers, the focus of the boot camp was to provide the fundamental tools and techniques for public speaking. The participants were given an opportunity to design, develop and deliver a 3 to 5 minutes' speech in public. Although it was the first attempt for many of the participants, the facilitators' guidance had inspired and guided them to speak in public with confidence. 20 participants from the boot camp were selected to attend a special workshop. Conducted for 5 sessions with 4 hours per session from December 2017 to March 2018, the objective of the workshop was to furnish the participants with knowledge to further enhance their ability to speak confidently in public. To make it more interesting, the workshop ended with a public speaking competition held on 25 March 2018 which was attended by their parents, giving the parents a chance to witness their children's 'transformation'. From being shy and having introverted personalities, the participants transformed themselves into being confident even in the face of the public, a fact which made both the facilitators and the Speak Eazy team proud of their efforts in 'giving a voice' to these teenagers.

Part of the Speak Eazy programme's participants and facilitators

BIG HEARTS

Uma Shangery Aruldass, a project engineer by profession and Priyaa Tharisiny Aruldass, a digital marketing executive are two of the core members of the Speak Eazy programme. An interesting fact about Uma and Priyaa is that they are siblings and their aspiration for joining the programme had come from their parents who are friends of Dr. Praba. "Before I decided to join this programme, I went to Speak Eazy a few times. Looking at the little brothers and sisters melted my heart as they are very loving and sweet. I believe that even if they don't have parents to rely on, I can contribute and help them. Once they reach a certain age, they will leave the orphanage house, and I suppose with proper training, they can have a bright and beautiful future", said Priyaa. Uma who was raised in the same home with Priyaa had a different story behind her motivation to help the underprivileged kids. "Our mother came from a poor family, a family that was really poor to the extent that she had to share a single meal with 7 other siblings and live in a very small house with a roofless toilet in a tiny village. Even though her fate has changed, her stories on how difficult it was for her to grow up had always aspired me to help others".

"In todays' era, it's very easy and there's lot of ways to contribute to people, even from a far. If you can't give money, contribute your knowledge. Just go and search for it, you will find such a platform. What you just need to have is a pure heart."

CATCHING KIDS' ATTENTION

"Managing the 5 to 12 years old kids is not easy, especially when it comes to making them listen to the teachers. However, the case is harder for teenagers as they are generally naughtier, are not able to focus on a topic for a long time, and spend a lot of time daydreaming. Thus, it is our responsibility to channel all their energy to the right ways such as public speaking", said Priyaa. To make the programme more interesting to the teenagers, Speak Eazy had organised different interesting games and other fun sessions for them. The team even used different approaches for different groups of kids. To attract the teenagers, Dr. Praba appointed Uma to lead the team by giving her the responsibility to expand the programme in order to attract more teenagers to join.

PriyaaTharisinyAruldass while facilitating a programme

THE CHALLENGES

Continuing and expanding the programme is a real challenge. Resources such as time, money and people are indeed limited. To ensure that the programme continues to run smoothly, Dr. Praba and his team tries to secure sponsorships from various companies; the donations received are used for their planned programmes' expenses. Finding the suitable time to conduct programmes is another challenge faced by the team, particularly due to the fact that all of them have their own full-time jobs. Despite several challenges, the team regularly conducts video and phone calls to discuss strategies and tactics that can be adopted to further enhance the programme.

As the programme expands, a bigger number of volunteers and teachers will be needed. However, Dr. Prabarealises that with the limited financial resources available, it is tough for the team to find volunteers, especially among the young generations.

FUTURE PLANS

Dr. Praba has big plans for the future. As he wants to reach out to more underprivileged kids, he has devised a lot of expansion plans. For example, he wants to expand Speak Eazy via the franchising method by developing his own modules. He also plans to obtain his own resources, collaborate with other non-governmental organisations, and conduct training for newly-appointed volunteers and teachers. With his one big mission of contributing and giving back to the society, Dr. Praba believes that he can bring Speak Eazy to greater heights.

Too Fast And Furious? A Malaysian Maverick's Blockchain Saga

Founder	:	Muhd. Azrainuddin Zainal (Arai Ezzra)
Nationality	:	Malaysian
Age of the founder at start-up	:	36
Education	:	Foundation Certificate in Information Technology
Professional background	:	Computer Programmer Trading Platform Developer System Developer
Family background	:	Malaysian The eldest of 4 siblings. Married with 4 daughters.
Business type	:	Financial Technology
Business partner	:	Rht Law. Oodles. Sk Consulting. Nuspay. Miranz.
Country of operation	:	Singapore, Malaysia, Japan, Indonesia, Thailand and London
Year of startup	:	2016

Written by:
Rahayu Tasnim

"In less than two years, we have established seven global offices in Japan, Bangkok, Singapore, Cambodia, Indonesia, Hong Kong, and soon UK and Dubai. We targeted this, but didn't want to grow too fast. Wanted to move stably...in control, but obviously...we... grew too fast. Too fast. [This] made us...scared".

Muhd Azrainuddin Zainal @ Arai Ezzra
Chairman of the Malaysian Association
Financial Technology Industry (MAFTI)
December 2016 – present

Stylishly stepping out from his posh, all- black and deeply tinted wagon, Muhd Azrainuddin Zainal, or popularly known in the financial world as Arai Ezzra, was then swiftly ushered into the lobby by two masculine-looking men in black shirts and sunglasses. Without a doubt, any sight of Arai would make heads turn, especially when accompanied by his eye-catching and charismatic wife, who once was attached to a media firm and appreciated modelling in her younger days. While Arai was cautiously being led to the building entrance, two younger men, cladded in black and blue shirts, punctually carted a bulky high definition movie camera and a chunky microphone ahead of Arai's steps. Then out came another young lad transporting a standing pod with two brightly lit, white coloured spotlights.

They began videotaping his elegant entrance.

It was always about these limelight moments that make Arai (and wife) a signature, and envy, of spectators. Accompanied by bodyguards, movie cameras and spotlights in almost every public appearance, it would be hard for people to ignore the glitzy hype created. The sight of bodyguards encircling you wherever you go signals an instantaneous assumption; (i) that somehow, you're non-typical (ii) that somehow, you're exclusive, and (iii) that somehow, you're affluent. In short, people see you as someone different.

With head held high, Arai graciously walked into the hall.

THE WILD BEGINNING AND PERSONAL VENDETTAS

It was in 2014 when the birth of a small IT firm in Kuala Lumpur was chronicled. Like other small IT start-ups gearing up for a competitive advantage, this small firm too was similarly servicing on app (applications) creations, web-based systems and in particular, financial applications. With 10 staff, Arai founded this firm to cater to the worldwide demand of financial based applications. This Kuala Lumpur based stint paved ways for Arai to gain new insights into how financial technology (fintech) is game-changing the world's economic landscape, pushing him to strongly believe on his capabilities of making his own mark in the aggressively competitive market. He has always believed in his talents. He believes in making changes and somehow, in solving the community's problems. And as Arai has always been known as, he dreams to succeed all these in stylish glamour. It was an unforgettable, painful, bumpy ride though, and the Kuala Lumpur start-up was not his first attempt on building his dreams.

It was Indonesia that gave him a wild start.

A few years earlier, Arai noticed an uptrend in online gold and silver trading in Indonesia. He was so overwhelmed by that fact that he decided to move to Bandung, bringing his family along. At this point, his vision was to stay put in Indonesia, and more importantly, to build his own global financial empire. From this point onwards, there was no turning back; even to the extent of him being detained for fraud and scam, or even after knowing that his own father conspired to topple him (he lost RM30 million in this personal vendetta!). With an estimated worth of RM100 million in his business equity, the game began to change faster than he could have imagined. Controversies, sabotage and hate campaigns were among the battles he had to face, almost daily. The Indonesian stint did not last long though and this was when he decided to return home.

THE CURIOUS MAVERICK AND THE GAME OF SCAMS

Back in the early 2000s, Arai served as a programmer in Kuala Lumpur. His passion and intelligence drove him to create a multitude of financial systems. However, a singular problem cutting across the systems he created probed him to move a step ahead from the rest of the programmers in his team; it was the hacking problem. He noticed this critical issue faced by banks and decided to look into the concept of blockchain technology. It was here that he learnt the potential of blockchain and how it is said to disrupt not only the financial sectors, but all sectors worldwide.

"And so I thought...if I don't grab this opportunity, I'd lose out!"

And he was right.

He reminisced the time when he was 14 and owned his first computer, bought by his parents. And he was hooked ever since;

"Since then, I was curious. How can I create games? IRC channels? Compared to the rest….as users".

Curiosity, to him, has always been his way of life.

"I'm not saying I'm good (compared to other programmers out there), but I can say I'm able to identify problems, solve and identify opportunities. If something appears and comes, I'm always firstly skeptical. It's the curiosity [in me]".

Having not brought up in a business environment (his parents were not into business), his education background, he claimed, is somewhat modest. Albeit scoring well in the Malaysian Education Certificate (SPM), he did not opt for a matriculation post (although he was a science student), but took up a foundation certificate from a local private university instead. Scoring the Dean's list award for the 1-year programme, and having been financially supported by Dana Ehsan (a state-government foundation) for a RM300 monthly allowance, he then left the formal education landscape and performed hands-on programming. In the next few years, he learnt and practiced paid programming, while the curiosity flame inside him continued to burn, yearning to know more. Craving for a vision. A personal vision.

Little did he know what was coming next.

It was in 2003 when the significant eureka episode happened. This was when his then girlfriend (soon-to-be wife) was scammed and instantly (in 5 seconds, in fact!) lost RM16,000 to a foreign exchange company. This triggered him to think, again out of deep curiosity;

> "How was it that we were scammed? What system was used? What app? ....and this was when I decided to learn trading [emphasised]".

Things went well subsequently, albeit for a short while. With his dynamic and curious personality, he was soon after awarded the best forex broker in 2008. But then, another scam episode played a major turn off; this time, it was his mother who faced an excruciating sting of a whopping RM500,000 loss. To him, it was episodes like these which brought the entire family together. Perseverance was key.

The years 2005 to 2009 then saw him breaking off from formal employment, opting for more flexible freelance programming works. He was doing fairly good, raking in no less than RM10,000 per month in programming projects. It was in this short period too that the world witnessed a breakthrough and an astounding point-of-departure from the traditional financing system: bitcoin was stylishly introduced for the first time in history. In next to no time, his curiosity in bitcoin tempted him to experiment with it himself. He became one of the pioneer investors of bitcoin in Malaysia. Little did he know that this wild move would make him a prominent multi-millionaire in less than a few years. One thing he did know though; that at that point he ingeniously predicted the crash of the Malaysian Ringgit.

It was later in 2011 that he noticed, and a turning point it became, that there was a plethora of Ponzi schemes in the market. These Ponzi schemes run comparably similar business models, often involving online gold-backed investments, boasting money-spinning returns. These "money games" promote "investors" to buy gold, only seeing them left weeping without any in the end. It was a devastating thought, not only for him, but for the thousands who were crying empty-handed. To him, a solution must be found. Fast.

THE MALAYSIAN LANDSCAPE: A BLOCKCHAIN BROUHAHA?

Thankfully, the Indonesian vendettas he faced did not last long. It was money and greed which prompted the series of personal attacks in Bandung, and he eventually decided to step out of this ecosystem, returning to Kuala Lumpur and re-strategise his moves. Indeed, the lesson he learnt in Indonesia was a painful one, which soon became a mantra to him and family (at this point, he was no longer acquainted to his biological father because of the father-son "conspiracy", but was very close with his mother). This mantra would soon echo throughout the rest of his entrepreneurial journey: "never trust anyone".

Returning to Kuala Lumpur in 2014 was not an easy task. Funds were short because of the millions he lost in Indonesia, so coming up with a new business plan was not as simple as he thought it would be. At this juncture, Ponzi schemes made headlines in almost all major newspapers and media. He quickly noted that in Malaysia, people love buying gold. The main pain point is, gold is difficult to sell; its spread is 20% to 30% less, with sellers bearing the cost. Hence he observed people storing gold in their houses instead, which is truly a chancy move.

"On the other hand, if one stores gold at a pawnshop, more will be spent. So where's the practicability in all these?"

And so he brilliantly created the DinarCoin.

The dinar coin

However, DinarCoin did not kickstart via the easy way. Upon returning to Kuala Lumpur, he set up a new company, FXBitLab, and focused on blockchain technology. It was at this point that he was starting to understand how blockchain would revolutionalise the fintech sector and other sectors as well. His small team started to experiment with blockchain projects, learning as much as they could from various global blockchain experts.

"It was really, really tough to find local blockchain experts! We scouted everywhere! Universities, professors, ...nobody knew what blockchain is. Even [on] Bitcoin too! What more to find local experts! Many claim they know what it is, but when it comes to the technical part, algorithms....I had to secure foreign programmers, mainly from India, Bangladesh, UK and Singapore, for my projects".

Never had his curiosity been at the highest apex. He did not leave home for six months because he was ultimately engrossed with his blockchain curiosity.

"Back then, I really knew next to nothing about blockchain! I started from zero!"

While he was eagerly learning about blockchain, the bitcoin and cryptocurrency market began to flourish. Whether it was out of mere curiosity and experimentation, or out of courageous investment predictions, more people are jumping onto the crypto-bandwagon. In less than no time, a multitude of new cryptocurrencies were being introduced and the cryptocurrency exchanges were hyped with activity. This was it. The world has begun to notice that the cryptocurrency market could no longer be ignored.

Arai had noticed this far earlier than the world did. Somehow he had predicted this. And so, carefully placing the jigsaw pieces together, he risked another colossal, bold move. This time, he placed himself straight onto the cryptocurrency industry "chessboard", head-to-head with the crypto-giants themselves.

A newcomer. A Malaysian. Using blockchain, of course, as the enabler.

Arai was not sure of how he would fare with DinarCoin (DNC), but he took all odds. He was running out of funds and needed a product that could win the hearts of thousands, if not millions of people worldwide.

"To sustain a successful business, we need to create future products' needs, not on the current needs. What's next in four to five years? What is needed? So we created a solution which allows gold to be spent [used] in small amounts; hence, DinarCoin. It's a one-to-one digital pack".

As soon as DNC was launched in 2016, Brunei became DNC's main supporter. This did not come as a huge shock to Arai's team, as he knew the characteristics of Bruneians: they are very into gold-based investments, and with the introduction of DNC, Bruneians are free to trade and spend gold in miniature amounts. Soon after, news on DNC spread to other parts of Borneo, and within two years, to other ASEAN nations. In less than two years, there were already 110,000 users on DNC's platform, spanning from no less than 10 countries. In October 2016, DNC was acknowledged by the biggest China Forex Expo as the "most innovative gold fintech provider". When this was launched, the Malaysian media was there and they soon heralded DNC as an innovation which "made Malaysia proud". One of the headlines even chanted "Malaysian now standing tall in China". In the months to come, Arai and team were busy coping with invitations to speak (as guest speakers, etc.) in top-notch world class fintech gatherings, including in London, Dubai, Japan and Singapore. The fintech world has started to acknowledge his talents while prominent collaborative offers too began flowing in.

"Amongst the undreamed-of offers were from Western Union and a Swiss-based bank".

But the personal mantra kept on echoing inside him. Although having been offered to sell his business for a multimillion dollar price tag, the mantra remained strong in him. Never trust anyone.

"Besides, this is my dream! How could I sell my dream? This isn't because of money, or getting rich, or recognition, this is because we'd like to make changes to the ecosystem. Solve people's problems".

As of today, his team has expanded wings to establish offices in Japan, Bangkok, Singapore, Cambodia, Indonesia, Hong Kong, and soon UK and Dubai.

Having being mentioned as a heroic Malaysian overseas, back home, things are not catching up as planned. Malaysia lacks the ecosystem to make cryptocurrencies a standing industry on its own. Policy-makers are playing safe by claiming blockchain and cryptocurrencies to be still in "infant stages" and that businesses starting up in these platforms are less encouraged compared to other fintech methodologies.

"On a talk to 100 lecturers, I asked, no one knew about blockchain and even Bitcoin. Only one or two did. So, that was where we knew in Malaysia, the awareness is near zero".

It sounded superbly ironic to Arai that while he is being mentioned in other regions of the world, back home however, "nobody seemed to know how to help". People became more sceptical because they did not know the fundamentals of these technologies and products. In Malaysia, there are still no laws on cryptocurrencies, and businesses could not even register for a private limited ownership with a crypto product (FXBitLab had to be registered in Singapore). According to Arai, Malaysia would like to support the cryptocurrency industry, but does not know how to start doing so. He remembered trying to talk to the local ministries about this, but was delicately shoveled out of their offices with statements like "Malaysia will be ready for the blockchain revolution by 2025" and "Is this another Ponzi scheme?". While Arai's team is being welcomed overseas, especially in Singapore, Dubai, Japan and Brunei, his hometown inhabitants still could not get it.

"The Dubai government even invited us in 2017 to contribute to Dubai's vision to ensure all documentations in blockchain format by 2020! This is it, I figured. I was born for this. I need to make my people learn about what I'm doing. About what other people from other parts of the world are banking on. I pity my people. [They are] so left out".

Arai laments that while other governments are investing in revolutionary technologies such as blockchain, Malaysia is still banking on the utilisation of the multimillions of dollars invested in infrastructure (most of these infrastructures according to him are not even fully utilised to date!). A simple example is the online banking infrastructure.

"We are still at the stage of promoting online banking, while others are leaping onto the more futuristic innovations! Like blockchain of course! I guess that's why MIGHT [Malaysian Industry-Government Group for High Technology] announced that Malaysia will be ready for these sort of evolutions only in 2025. And I thought...hey...they're right!".

But his team carried on, in its own way, speaking at local universities, organising international gatherings and aggressively promoting the technology in the local media. Arai's wife was once attached to the media, hence allowing for ample opportunities for the team to be heard and watched on national TV and radio channels, social and printed media. While these awareness and educational contributions to the public became a passionate practice of Arai and team, specific focus on other administrative matters was crucially needed. With offices abroad and an increasing staff count in their Kuala Lumpur office (more than 70 staff in KL), attention was needed on strategic planning and on their next moves.

"At times, we are lost. Things are moving so fast. People are looking for us, from all parts of the world. But we need to focus. Maybe...we're moving too fast".

While the internal affairs of FXBitLab became a major concern to Arai, the local financial institutions started to feel threatened by Arai's capabilities. According to Arai, the local banks are five to six times behind when it comes to technology. To him, for banks to change to a newer system would take a long time. Yes, there are companies championing blockchain technology in Malaysia, but these are foreign companies branching out to the ASEAN markets.

"No local companies have succeeded this far. We are born global".

It was an entirely different phenomenon altogether in Singapore though. To Arai, Singapore is somewhat "special". It does not regulate cryptocurrencies, neither bans it. Hence any cryptocurrency related start-up is allowed to be formed and run in Singapore, resulting in a flourishing number of innovative companies on the bitcoin exchanges. This very interesting phenomenon attracted Arai and team to establish BCMY (Blockchains. my), aiming to become one of the world's blockchain service providers. To him, Singapore offers more than just a posh corporate office setting; it offers support in many ways when it comes to innovative start-ups in fintech.

While BCMY is being set up in the heart of the Singaporean metropolis, Arai feels the heighted pressure to support potential Malaysian start-ups venturing into fintech markets. In next to no time, Blockspace and Blockcafé were launched in Kuala Lumpur to house potential fintech start-ups under one roof. Blockspace applies the co-working space ecosystem, similar to the ones in Silicon Valley and Google Campuses. It houses more than 20 shared working spaces in a 4-storey building, along with working lounges and private meeting rooms. This creates a synergistic ecosystem where resources, support and network are shared. Blockcafé is an exclusive, informal hangout hub situated on the ground floor of Blockspace, and is open to the public. Apart from a chic bar, it houses a sophisticated mini theatre which can house up to 170 audience. Both Blockspace and Blockcafe aim to become a one-stop centres for blockchain and fintech conversations, bonding local fintech start-ups and their networks in the process.

Blockspace and Blockcafe

THE MAVERICK HAS IT ALL

Arai sees the upward trend in fintech start-ups these days, but is still sceptical on the support from the local fintech (including legal, etc.) ecosystem. Nonetheless, he is confident that as time comes, Malaysia can no longer play wait-and-see, and that when the nation notices this, Arai and team will be happy to support all they can to guide Malaysia on how to stay in tandem with the fintech revolution. On his personal advice to Malaysians who dream to start-up in fintech, he says;

1. "Just do it!"
2. "Something big is happening…and this something will change our daily lives. The blockchain revolution will become even larger than the internet!"
3. "Venture capitalists no longer invest in conventional start-ups. They go for blockchain start-ups. Just look at Singapore, billions of dollars have gone into blockchain based start-ups. More than 300 blockchain start-ups have secured funds!"

4. "Financial institutions may have already created their blockchain departments or units, and they need expertise to build blockchain based applications. This is creating an explosion of apps!"
5. "So, if you were to ask me, must we stop the fintech revolution? No, we can't! It's even open-sourced!"

"If a small guy like me can do this and am being highly acknowledged in Japan, Dubai and in other parts of the world, anyone can do so too. We're not saying that we are proud of ourselves; however, this clearly showed us that our technology and capability are transferable to the more developed nations! Rather than what is being done ...the other way around. Oh, and we're not scared of competition too. The more and tougher the playing field is, the better room for improvements and innovation. Being ten years ahead in terms of technology, I believe we're moving fast...although struggling...but we're on the right track".

With the upcoming launch of a new cryptocurrency backed by gold, and with a long list of clients waiting to gain insights from his blockchain services and solutions, Arai and team have it all. A lengthy list of challenges awaits him too. Nevertheless, being Arai, and after all that he has gone through, nothing is impossible.

But still a mix of feelings haunt him.

Restlessness? Disturbed? Fulfilled? Deprived?

A maverick will need to deal with this, he thought. No matter what.

Imaginary Pay

Founder	:	Pak Loong Chan
Nationality	:	Malaysian
Age of the founder at start-up	:	33
Education	:	BSc Software Engineering
Professional background	:	Software Engineer
Family background	:	Education
Business type	:	Financial Technology
Work experience	:	10.5 years at HSBC
Country of operation	:	Malaysia
Year of startup	:	2015

Written by:
Zarina Abdul Salam

BUSINESS INSPIRATION

Pak Loong Chan studied Software Engineering and worked in the Hong Kong and Shanghai Banking Corporation (HSBC) as a software engineer for more than ten years, and he gained a lot of experiences while working in HSBC. One of his responsibilities was handling payment services with some international banks located in South Korea, Japan and Thailand. The countries that he was in charge with gave him the exposure that there were so many differences in processing transactions for these countries; for example, different vendors, different processing systems used, different time and dates, different regulations, different culture and different languages from end to end. Due to these differences, there were many difficulties that arose such as delays in receiving payment from customers, waiting approval for money transfer the next working day or the following week due to time differences, interruption in receiving goods from suppliers due to incomplete documentations required by different countries, etc. Delays in receiving goods or services and unprompt payments from customers would irritate users and make them seek for a system that will process financial transactions promptly and deliver the goods and services on time.

Another important thing that Chan noticed was that financial institutions need to upgrade their regulations from time to time due to risky incidences that may impact payment services such as in the September 11 attack in the USA. Many banks had imposed new and stricter regulations due to such incidences apart from the rapid growth of technology system. Therefore, local banks need to upgrade their regulations almost every year to keep updated with the regulations set by international banks that they dealt with. This is very hectic and not an easy task because changing regulations for one country costs the bank at least

USD 15,000 as there are many international banks from various countries that the bank dealt with. Sometimes Chan had to go to these countries to discuss the inconsistencies in the banking regulations and was required to make an agreement with the bankers and prospect users. There were also times where inconsistencies of regulations could not be solved immediately and more time was needed to see the impact to both sides if decisions were to be made. Pak Loong Chan sat on a sofa and had a deep thought about how to solve this problem.

"How can I make life easier for everybody in making financial transactions? The customers keep complaining about the delay in receiving goods and services that they purchased, the sellers complained of the delay in receiving payment from customers, and sometimes issues arose where customers claimed that they had made the payment, but the sellers claimed that they had not received it. How to solve these issues?"

With ten years of experience in HSBC and education and knowledge in Software Engineering, Chan thought of introducing a new user-friendly financial application that will solve all the differences, ease users in dealing with financial transactions anytime and anywhere, and also minimise the required and complex documentations that will irritate the application's users. This application was named as "Imaginary pay" because the founders wanted the application to be able to do what they have imagined in their minds and they wanted to make them a reality. The newly-introduced application will make life easier for users and can change himself better rather than put this knowledge to waste. However, the financial application that he set up needed tight security and up-to-date technology to make the system reliable and attractive to users. Chan did not propose the application to the banking industry because they were not interested to do this sort of application as they are focused more on other types of businesses that can generate greater profitability.

Pak Loong Chan, the founder of Imaginary Pay

THE BUSINESS SERVICES

The internet is one of the greatest creations as it allows people to communicate and share endless information around the world instantly. The internet has also revolutionised the way of shopping, which is from conventional to online shopping, where anyone with internet access is able to buy products that they wished to have without having to visit any stores. The internet provides easy access to compare prices of the same products by different companies and online reviews to help customers make better purchasing decisions. When a purchase is made, the payment of goods and services is made online by transferring money from customers to sellers. Online purchase is very convenient. However, the payment system's security has been a concern to customers as there have been many fraudulent transactions taking place, with customers' accounts being hacked, thus leading to financial losses. Financial crime had increasingly become a concern to the government and financial institutions throughout the world. Financial crime is defined as any kind of criminal conduct related to money or the financial services or markets including offences such as fraud or dishonesty and misconduct or misuse of information relating to financial markets. Financial crime has become an important issue because it is a substantial threat to the development of economies and countries stability.

The vision of Chan's company is to harmonise the world's money transfer and payment. Money transfer and payment for local transactions can be easily carried out. Money transfer for international transactions however involves more documents and many intermediaries, asthere is a lot of paperwork to be prepared. The mission of this company is to develop a user-friendly payment service to help people with money transfers or payments.

Imaginary pay was developed to act as a platform for customers to pay without much hassle. For example, different traders use different financial institutions for payment services and these financial institutions have different regulations which would delay the payments. Currently, traders are using financial institution's system to pay. It would be more convenient for customers to pay using imaginary pay because of the time difference between countries. If the customers want to buy products internationally and the involved financial institutions have already closed their operations, they have to wait for the next working day or the following week for the payments to be settled due to the time difference between countries. Therefore, this may cause a delay in receiving the products ordered.

FUNDING THE BUSINESS

"How to run the business? I am short of cash. I need at least RM 2 million to run this business. What am I going to do? Am I going to borrow from the bank? Definitely not. I have to pay at least 5 million if I borrow from the bank."

Chan discussed with his family and closest friends on the best way to raise money for the business. As Chan has worked in the banking industry for more than ten years, he knew that borrowing from financial institutions would give a big impact to the company to pay the interests, especially for a new start-up company. Chan might not be able to borrow as the bank also requires mortgage equivalent to the amount that he wanted to borrow. After deep thinking, Chan decided to share the company's capital with his brother, Seng Loong Chan and his closest friend, ManigandanRaju, who were then appointed as the co-founders of the company. Still, the company is short of cash. They had to limit the risk of putting every asset that they owned to prevent them from bankruptcy. Therefore, they decided to start fundraising to get contributions from other resources, such as donations, individual businesses, charitable foundations and governmental agencies. They also came up with capital sharing from trustable professionals.

Chan and all the co-foundersbelieved that Imaginary Pay application would be a success in the future despite money shortages. Therefore, they are taking several steps to minimise expenses. There was no office set up for the company due to budget constraints, hence founder and co-founders worked from home.

BUSINESS OPERATIONS

Related education and working experience in HSBC provide many advantages to Chan to handle business operations. Chan planned to converge and avoid multi system that would delay the process of purchasing by customers and the sellers to receive payments. The imaginary application was constructed and to save cost, the application system was designed to be autonomous and transactions were being screened, identified and processed through automation means. Having autonomous application made Chan and all the co-founders worked from home to save cost. They do not have to recruit employees to run the business. If there were any unusual transactions or problems, the system would alert Chan and the co-founders to take actions. They would look at the matter and choose either to proceed or discontinue the transaction. The founders would look at the results of business operations every month, made analysis and made decisions for improvement.

The Imaginary pay application provides benefits for its users. For example, users need not inform the system if they wanted to use this application abroad. Some financial institutions require users to inform them before payment is made abroad, as an additional security. All transactions that went through this application would be stored securely at Amazon, Google and Cloud of which Chan had paid reasonable fees. This company has an infinite storage of secured business data. Therefore, there is no limit of users to use this financial application.

BUSINESS COMPETITORS

Competitors are getting smarter and they hit the market with new and exciting products that captured customers' interests. There are many companies that offer faster, cheaper and more transparent payments which have created pressures for the banks to innovate new services. The merger and acquisition of several financial applications would also give pressure to smaller companies, especially new companies that have recently been formed. Some of the established payment applications used in Malaysia are Cash, Samsung Pay, Alipay, PayPal, WeChat Pay, MOL Pay, Grab Pay and Ta Pay. Grab Pay initially allowed Grab users to enjoy cashless payments for transportation. Grab Pay had since extended their services by incorporating other payment services apart from Grab rides. In the future, Grab users may also purchase goods and services from this application and may also make money transfers to relatives and friends. Grab Pay is waiting for approval from the Central Bank of Malaysia (BNM) to provide such services. MOL Pay is popular for younger generations where they neither have credit nor debit card to purchase, yet to also make convenient cashless payment. MOL Pay users will pay cash at various 7-Eleven stores in Malaysia and the users can make payment online by using this application.

CHALLENGES AHEAD

As there are many financial application services, how to attract customers?

> "How to increase customers? What do they want? What are the unique services that has never been offered by other financial payment application to be offered to users ?"

Currently, there are four types of customers for the application that Chan had developed which are end-customers, merchants, financial institutions and developers. Developer is similar to merchants, but the difference is that developer uses hashtag to trade their products, for example Alibaba and Rakuten. There are around 200-300 end-customers and 10 – 20 merchants.

Chan believed that trust is very important and may influence customers to use the imaginary pay application. Bank Negara Malaysia had been requested to approve him a license to operate as a financial technology company and to enhance customers' trust towards the payment application that they had set up. This company had also joined the Swiss Innovation Challenge Asia (SIC) held by the Azman Hashim International Business School (AHIBS) to accelerate the business progress and hopefully increase the number of customers in the long term.

BUSINESS IN THE FUTURE?

Financial applications have to be innovative and competitive for survival in the industry. The application needs to be developed according to users' needs and demands. Successful innovations not only respond to current customers' needs but also anticipate future trends and ideas that will meet future demand effectively. Chan needs to update its application progressively.

Malaysia Rare Disorders Society (MRDS): A Golden Citizen's Struggle

Founder	:	Dato' Hatijah Ayob
Nationality	:	Malaysian
Age of the founder at start-up	:	60
Professional background	:	Human resource manager, Harper Gilfillan (M) SdnBhd Executive Secretary, Heart Foundation of Malaysia President for Malaysian Women's Action for Tobacco Control and Health (MyWATCH) Founder, Chairperson and President, Malaysia Rare Disorder Society (MRDS)
Family background	:	Hospital staffs, social activists
Organisation type	:	Non-governmental Organisation (NGO)
Country of operation	:	Malaysia
Year of commencement	:	2004

Written by:
Muhammad Nizam Zainuddin & Obed Rashdi Syed

ABOUT THE FOUNDER

Dato' Hatijah Ayob comes from a family of eight siblings. Being in a big family teaches her several good values such as *'sharing is caring'* and *'togetherness through the thick and thin'*. Her parents used to work as support personnel at Ipoh General Hospital in Perak, Malaysia. Since her childhood, she has witnessed her parents' interests and involvement in social activities much related to the local working-class community.

Dato' Hatijah's father was an active union member who strived for fair treatment of hospital staffs who performed their duties around the clock. Her father used to share with her about his daily routines in the hospital. She still remembered on one beautiful day, her father shared a heart-breaking story about an unfortunate patient who experienced an unknown life-threatening illness. That story though remains fresh in her mind, it reminds her about the difficulties faced by the patient's family members in accepting the patients' health condition.

Dato' Hatijah Ayob, the founder of Malaysia Rare Disorders Society

The idea of helping unfortunate individuals further emerged and getting more profound when she witnessed how her daughter, Jasmin, and her son-in-law, Remei struggled when the couple had two children who were diagnosed with a rare disorder called Congenital Disorders of Glycosylation (CDG) Type 1a. She observed the anger and resentment initially felt by Jasmin. She witnessed closely how her daughter was torn between caring for a sick baby, Aminisha and trying to live a regular life as a working mother. Dato' Hatijah observed Jasmin's constant emotional burden in her efforts to find the best way to take care of her sick baby, as deep inside she knew that Aminisha was living a short, borrowed time.

"My intention to help others evolves when my granddaughter was diagnosed with a congenital disorder. She was constantly warded, and I see there are a lot of people with disorder children are upset and guilty. ... So, I want to lessen their burden."

Dato' Hatijah's beloved granddaughter, Aminisha, passed away at seven months old. A few years later, Jasmin gave birth to another baby, Ali Bahatiar, who was healthy as he did not have the CDG type 1a, but he was a carrier. This time around, Jasmin was prepared; she quit her job and tried her best to take care of her son. Dato' Hatijah's grandson went for regular checks to monitor his growth and development. A few years later, Jasmin had another baby, Ali Zulfiqar, but he shared a similar condition with his late sister, Aminisha. The unfortunate baby passed away at five months old. Dato' Hatijah was heartbroken by the tragedy, and this became the trigger that motivated her to form a non-governmental society where she can channel her grief into a positive energy to help those in the same shoes with her and Jasmin.

FOUNDATION OF THE MALAYSIA RARE DISORDERS SOCIETY (MRDS)

With the passion and willingness to help the niche society of rare disorders patients and their immediate family members, Dato' Hatijah began to develop an extensive social networking circle with individuals in the corporate sector and social activists in community organisations. Her aim was to establisha strong network that can help her to realise her idea of helping people.

MRDS commenced its operations in 2004 with the support and guidance of the Department of Paediatrics, the University of Malaya Medical Centre, Kuala Lumpur, Malaysia. It is led by Dato' Hatijah and a group of individuals, including a research professor from Universiti Malaya. They share the same vision and aspiration to serve and support unfortunate families whose child or family member is suffering from a rare disorder. They established an organisation called *"Persatuan Penyakit Jarang Jumpa"*, which in English means *"Malaysia Rare Disorders Society"* (MRDS), with the motive of facilitating the rare disorder patients to have the opportunity and accessibility to proper healthcare and quality of life.

"We [the group] do whatever we can, wherever we can have [the] opportunity. So, we started this [MRDS], but we didn't know where and how to do it. So we have to create something. We started this society, so we have to support one and another to support those patients."

The establishment of the organisation faced challenges from the beginning. Although she had a group of well-established people who willingly supported her and were aspired by her ideas, but it was hard to identify and locate the patients. Initially, she reached out to families whose members were suffering from the rare disorder. She was able to persuade them to join MRDS.

To increase awareness in the society, Dato' Hatijah launched the MRDS website and worked closely with 10 newly registered rare disease organisations and a few support groups. She also sought support from the ministries to help her in spreading awareness of rare disorders to the society. In the first 10 years, her efforts were solely devoted to creating awareness in the society.

"When we started, the first thing we did was the website. ... We see that there is no information on the disease, even the Ministry of Health has no database. They know it is there, but the number of patients, they say is sikit [small]. So we had to create an information. We registered [a website] as a society for the rare disease. ... Awareness is important, then they [patient's families] will come. Then we will connect with other parents who face [the] same problem. ... There are so many parents who have no information and no time to go outstation, so we had to do awareness programmes, and we meet ministries to seek support."

The foundation of MRDS was solely based on the principle of a *"voluntary support group"*. MRDS opened its doors to those who would contribute to help those families whose members suffer from rare diseases. As the founder, Dato' Hatijah specifically mentioned that *"I don't want to*

refer to them as our patients but our children. We need to help as they are unfortunate and experience challenges in life". To help the patients and families, Dato' Hatijah has structured four objectives for MRDS: 1) *to support and provide practical aid to individuals and families affected with rare disorders*; 2) *to increase awareness of rare disorders by providing information on rare disorders and educate individuals, families, medical professionals, schools, organisations, and the general public*; 3) *to establish a network between individuals and families with rare disorders with relevant organisations, professionals, education and intervention centres*; and 4) *to collaborate with organisations that have the potential to affirm, prevent, improve treatment and increase the quality of life of individuals affected with rare disorders*. By 2017, MRDS had more than 2000 patients and 70 types of rare condition diseases recorded in their database.

"Most of them have disabilities, sometimes not one but multiple, and sometimes they are diagnosed late, or they get the wrong diagnosis...We have to help one another; it's not just money, it's not just treatment. There are issues where they need moral support. Just listen to the mother, be there for them, and it helps a lot when you talk with parents who have all these problems."

CHALLENGES ENCOUNTERED

The formation of MRDS was not without its challenges. Maintaining the operation and sustaining the organization was difficult due to money factor, especially when the support funds were primarily meant to help those families whose members were suffering from rare disorder diseases. To ensure the smooth running of the organization, fundraising campaigns were initiated by distributing pamphlets to the public. In addition, MRDS had organised two national conferences on rare diseases to spread awareness, trigger interests, and gain support from relevant authorities and policymakers.

"Companies ask us how many people will benefit from our programme? Where will the children be treated?"

Money was not the only issue. MRDS also faced challenges in the implementation and management of the ideas. As an NGO that mainly relied on voluntary contributions from the members, motivating the members was hard because all of the members are professional people with a lot of commitments. There were some great ideas that remained just ideas due to the difficulties in getting support from all the members.

Educating the society was another issue. The society is well-versed about common diseases like diabetes, heart attack, AIDS, cancers and others, and medical sciences have proven remedies for these diseases. However, not many people are aware of the rare genetic disorders, as her grandchildren had suffered.

"Heart issues are different from genetic disorders. Let's say you have the heart problem in your child, you know it can be repaired, the whole heart can be repaired. But when it comes to genetic problem, it's difficult because that can cause other problems."

As disorder diseases are originated in the gene and are genetic in nature, they are often a life-threatening, untreatable, and chronically debilitating disease that may result beyond the imagination of individuals. Consequently, both the patient and the family suffer a lot.

"So much needs to be done for people with rare disorders, from reducing their cost of medication to acceptance into mainstream schools and palliative care. Parents also need help and counselling. Having a child with a rare disorder can drain you emotionally and financially, but MRDS is always there to help."

www.ingramcontent.com/pod-product-compliance
Lightning Source LLC
Chambersburg PA
CBHW020931180526
45163CB00007B/2968